Sneaky Press Word Puzzles

Puzzle Boxes

Volume 1

U	E	Z
Z	P	O
X	L	B

SNEAKY PRESS
©Copyright 2022
Pauline Malkoun

The right of Pauline Malkoun to be identified as author of this work has been asserted by them in accordance with Copyright, Designs and Patents Act 1988.

All Rights Reserved.

No reproduction, copy or transmission of this publication may be made without written permission. No paragraph of this publication may be reproduced, copied or transmitted save with the written permission of the publisher, or in accordance with the provisions of the Copyright Act 1956 (as amended).

Any person who commits any unauthorized act in relation to this publication may be liable to criminal prosecution and civil claims for damages.

A catalogue record for this work is available from the National Library of Australia.

ISBN 9781922641298

Sneaky Press is the imprint of Sneaky Universe.
www.sneakyuniverse.com
First published in 2022

Sneaky Press
Melbourne, Australia.

The Benefits of Word Puzzles

Not only are word puzzles fun but they are great for building literacy skills. They can help develop word recognition, pattern recognition, for example learning that usually, "i" comes before "e" and "q" is usually followed by "u" and word puzzles also help improve spelling, and expand vocabulary.

How to Complete a Puzzle Box

The goal is to write as many words (at least 3 letters) as you can using the 9 letters in each Puzzle Box including the 9 letter word. To make it a little easier a clue for the 9 letter word has been included with each puzzle and the 9 letter word always starts with the letter in the centre of the puzzle box. A target has also been included but feel free to go over it! Each letter in the puzzle box can only be used once in any words you identify. Of course if a letter is repeated in the puzzle box, each of these letters can be used in any words you identify. Solutions are in the back of this book and although they are substantial, you may find that you come up with words not listed—it doesn't matter, all words are acceptable and can contribute to your target.

Puzzle 1

D	N	E
D	A	O
A	B	N

Clue: To have left something /someone behind with no intention of returning for them/it.

Target: 30   9 letter word: _____

Other words:

Puzzle 2

O	A	T
N	D	T
P	I	A

Clue: A single piece of information.

Target: 30   9 letter word: _____

Other words:

Puzzle 3

P	S	A
A	S	E
C	U	N

Clue: A piece of kitchen equipment which usually has a long handle and lid used for cooking.

Target: 32   9 letter word: _____

Other words:

Puzzle 4

G	N	T
S	L	E
E	N	H

Clue: The act of making something longer.

Target: 30   9 letter word: _____

Other words:

Puzzle 5

R	R	A
E	C	K
A	T	E

Clue: A person responsible for the maintenance of a building or property.

Target: 32   9 letter word: _____

Other words:

Puzzle 6

L	A	L
E	F	E
S	R	W

Clue: Expressions of good wishes at departure.

Target: 32   9 letter word: _____

Other words:

_____ _____ _____ _____
_____ _____ _____ _____
_____ _____ _____ _____
_____ _____ _____ _____
_____ _____ _____ _____
_____ _____ _____ _____
_____ _____ _____ _____

Puzzle 7

I	S	F
R	O	G
P	N	F

Clue: The children or young of humans or an animal.

Target: 30   9 letter word: _____

Other words:

Puzzle 8

O	K	B
L	W	A
A	T	U

Clue: An informal public stroll taken by political figures or royalty to meet or be seen by the general public.

Target: 20   9 letter word: _____

Other words:

Puzzle 9

E	K	I
A	B	C
R	F	D

Clue: The sound made by a car which is not functioning correctly.

Target: 32   9 letter word: _____

Other words:

Puzzle 10

N	A	I
H	M	Y
E	C	R

Clue: Several large electric powered tools grouped together in one place.

Target: 32   9 letter word: _____

Other words:

Puzzle 11

E	A	T
G	O	P
R	I	N

Clue: Another word to describe a doctor performing surgery.

Target: 32   9 letter word: _____

Other words:

Puzzle 12

E	R	N
A	G	T
S	E	S

Clue: The quality of being important or distinguished.

Target: 32   9 letter word: _____

Other words:

Puzzle 13

R	E	A
B	J	B
N	I	G

Clue: Speaking quickly and incoherently.

Target: 30   9 letter word: _____

Other words:

Puzzle 14

E	C	E
L	C	L
D	N	A

Clue: When something which was going to take place is no longer going to take place.

Target: 24   9 letter word: _____

Other words:

Puzzle 15

O	A	E
S	S	S
R	H	E

Clue: Marine creatures which look a little like a land mammal often found on a farm.

Target: 32   9 letter word: _____

Other words:

Puzzle 16

O	A	R
G	K	O
N	S	A

Clue: Large jumping marsupials.

Target: 30   9 letter word: _____

Other words:

Puzzle 17

R	I	R
A	H	P
S	A	Y

Clue: Usually in an aerosol, this liquid holds hair in place after styling.

Target: 30   9 letter word: _____

Other words:

_____ _____ _____ _____
_____ _____ _____ _____
_____ _____ _____ _____
_____ _____ _____ _____
_____ _____ _____ _____
_____ _____ _____ _____
_____ _____ _____ _____

Puzzle 18

T	E	N
A	R	I
R	W	A

Clue: The substance that falls from clouds in the sky.

Target: 32   9 letter word: _____

Other words:

_____ _____ _____ _____
_____ _____ _____ _____
_____ _____ _____ _____
_____ _____ _____ _____
_____ _____ _____ _____
_____ _____ _____ _____
_____ _____ _____ _____
_____ _____ _____ _____

Puzzle 19

R	I	A
E	D	V
L	D	E

Clue: Someone who likes to partake in reckless and dangerous activities.

Target: 32   9 letter word: _____

Other words:

Puzzle 20

T	R	S
I	Y	D
A	K	C

Clue: A standard used to measure against.

Target: 32   9 letter word: _____

Other words:

_____ _____ _____ _____
_____ _____ _____ _____
_____ _____ _____ _____
_____ _____ _____ _____
_____ _____ _____ _____
_____ _____ _____ _____
_____ _____ _____ _____
_____ _____ _____ _____

Puzzle 21

S	M	R
E	I	O
T	P	S

Clue: People who pretend to be someone others.

Target: 32   9 letter word: _____

Other words:

Puzzle 22

R	U	A
T	Q	D
S	A	N

Clue: Multiple quarters of a circle.

Target: 30   9 letter word: _____

Other words:

_____ _____ _____ _____
_____ _____ _____ _____
_____ _____ _____ _____
_____ _____ _____ _____
_____ _____ _____ _____
_____ _____ _____ _____
_____ _____ _____ _____

Puzzle 23

I	T	N
A	E	H
G	R	L

Clue: An inhabitant on the third planet from the sun.

Target: 32   9 letter word: _____

Other words:

Puzzle 24

E	E	A
W	N	S
N	G	T

Clue: A small shop where daily newspapers can be purchased.

Target: 32   9 letter word: _____

Other words:

_____ _____ _____ _____
_____ _____ _____ _____
_____ _____ _____ _____
_____ _____ _____ _____
_____ _____ _____ _____
_____ _____ _____ _____
_____ _____ _____ _____
_____ _____ _____ _____

Puzzle 25

O	R	A
S	R	C
E	H	E

Clue: A very fast stallion or mare.

Target: 32   9 letter word: _____

Other words:

Puzzle 26

F	E	R
O	L	E
T	V	S

Clue: Food which has not been eaten and saved for a later meal.

Target: 32   9 letter word: _____

Other words:

_____   _____   _____   _____
_____   _____   _____   _____
_____   _____   _____   _____
_____   _____   _____   _____
_____   _____   _____   _____
_____   _____   _____   _____
_____   _____   _____   _____
_____   _____   _____   _____

Puzzle 27

E	N	O
N	S	D
A	T	S

Clue: A common type of sedimentary rock often found near water and deserts.

Target: 30   9 letter word: _____

Other words:

Puzzle 28

E	E	C
A	P	K
M	R	A

Clue: An electronic device that helps regulate heartbeat.

Target: 24   9 letter word: _____

Other words:

_____ _____ _____ _____
_____ _____ _____ _____
_____ _____ _____ _____
_____ _____ _____ _____
_____ _____ _____ _____
_____ _____ _____ _____
_____ _____ _____ _____
_____ _____ _____ _____

Puzzle 29

T	A	T
C	W	I
A	S	O

Clue: A garment for women similar to a vest worn in the 18th century when riding a horse.

Target: 30   9 letter word: _____

Other words:

_____ _____ _____ _____
_____ _____ _____ _____
_____ _____ _____ _____
_____ _____ _____ _____
_____ _____ _____ _____
_____ _____ _____ _____
_____ _____ _____ _____

Puzzle 30

P	O	E
R	T	D
S	A	R

Clue: Several small amounts of water that flow from the eye.

Target: 32   9 letter word: _____

Other words:

Solutions

Puzzle 1

9 Letter Word: Abandoned

Other Words: add, ado, and, baa, bad, ban, bed, boa, bod, dab, dad, den, doe, don, end, eon, nab, nan, nod, odd, ode, one, anon, bade, band, bane, bead, bean, bend, bode, bond, bone, dead, dean, done, naan, nada, neon, node, none, abode, anode, boded, boned, aboded, banded, banned, bonded, donned, abandon

Puzzle 2

9 Letter Word: Datapoint

Other Words: ado aid, and, ant, apt, din, dip, don, dot, ion, nap, nit, nod, not, oat, opt, pad, pan, pat, pin, pit, pod, pot, tad, tan, tap, tat, tin, tip, ton, top, tot, anti, atop, data, dint, into, iota, nada, paid, pain, pant, pint, pita, pond, tint, toad, adapt, adopt, ditto, inapt, paint, panda, patio, piano, pinot, pinto, point, taint, titan, attain, taipan, tinpot, adaption

Puzzle 3

9 Letter Word: Saucepans

Other Words: ace, ape, asp, can, cap, cue, cup, nap, pan, pea, pen, pun, sac, sap, sea, spa, sue, sun, ups, use, aces, acne, apes, asps, cane, cans, cape, caps, case, cues, cups, cusp, cuss, nape, naps, pace, pane, pans, pass, peas, pens, puns, puss, sane, sans, saps, scan, seas, snap, span, spun, sues, suns, uses, canes, capes, cases, cause, cusps, napes, paces, panes, passe, pause, pecan, sauce, sauna, scans, snaps, space, spans, canape, causes, census, nausea, pauses, pecans, sauces, saunas, scapes, spaces, canapes, nauseas, uncases, saucepan

Puzzle 4

9 Letter Word: Lengthens

Other Words: eel, gel, get, hen, let, net, see, set, she, tee, ten, the, eels, else, gels, gene, gent, gets, ghee, glee, glen, heel, hens, legs, lens, lent, lest, lets, nest, nets, seen, sent, teen, tees, tens, thee, then, genes, gents, heels, sheen, sheet, sleet, steel, teens, tense, these, gentle, length, nestle, lengths, lengthen

Puzzle 5

9 Letter Word: Caretaker

Other Words: ace, act, arc, are, ark, art, ate, car, cat, ear, eat, eek, era, err, rat, tar, tea, tee, acre, area, cake, care, cart, race, rack, rake, rare, rate, rear, reek, tack, take, tare, teak, tear, tree, trek, carat, carer, caret, carte, cater, crate, creak, creek, eater, erect, racer, react, taker, terra, track, aerate, career, carter, cerate, crater, create, errata, karate, racker, racket, rerack, retack, retake, retear, tracer, caterer, recrate, retaker, retrace, retrack, teacake, terrace, tracker, caretake

Puzzle 6

9 Letter Word: Farewells

Other Words: ale, all, are, awe, ear, eel, elf, era, ewe, far, fee, few, law, lea, lee, raw, saw, sea, see, sew, war, was, wee, ales, earl, ears, ease, eels, else, eras, ewes, fall, fare, fear, feel, fees, fell, flaw, flea, flee, flew, free, laws, leaf, leas, leer, lees, real, reef, reel, refs, safe, sale, seal, sear, seer, self, sell, serf, slaw, slew, wall, ware, wars, wear, wees, well, were, earls, easel, erase, falls, false, fares, fears, feels, fella, feral, fewer, flare, flaws, fleas, flees, frees, laser, lease, leers, reefs, reels, safer, sewer, swear, swell, wafer, walls, wares, wears, wells, fellas, flares, leaser, resale, reseal, resell, sealer, seller, wafers, weasel, welfare, farewell

Puzzle 7

9 Letter Word: Offspring

Other Words: fig, fin, fir, fog, for, gin, ion, nor, off, pin, pro, rig, rip, sin, sip, sir, son, figs, fins, firs, fogs, frog, grin, grip, info, ions, iron, noir, nori, pigs, ping, pins, pong, pros, riff, rigs, ring, rips, sign, sing, snip, snog, song, spin, frogs, giros, grins, grips, groin, irons, noirs, pings, pongs, prong, riffs, rings, sniff, spiff, sprig, groins, posing, prison, prongs, signor, soring, spring, spinoff, sporing

Puzzle 8

9 Letter Word: Walkabout

Other Words: baa, bat, boa, bot, bow, but, lab, law, lob, lot, low, oak, oat, out, owl, tab, tow, tub, two, wok, alto, auto, balk, bawl, blot, blow, boat, bolt, bout, bowl, bulk, lota, lout, talk, tuba, walk, about, bloat, koala, outlaw, outwalk, walkout

Puzzle 9

9 Letter Word: Backfired

Other Words: ace, aid, air, arc, are, ark, bad, bar, bed, bid, bra, cab, car, dab, dib, die, ear, era, fab, fad, far, fed, fib, fie, fir, ice, ire, irk, kid, rad, red, ref, rib, rid, aced, acid, acre, aide, arid, back, bade, bake, bard, bare, barf, bark, bead, beak, bear, bide, bike, bird, brae, bred, brie, cafe, cake, carb, card, care, crab, crib, dare, dark, deaf, dear, deck, dice, dire, drab, drib, face, fade, fair, fake, fare, fear, fire, iced, idea, kerb, race, rack, raid, rake, read, rice, ride, rife, abide, acrid, aider, aired, baked, baker, bared, beard, biked, biker, brace, braid, brake, bread, break, brick, bride, brief, caked, cared, cedar, cider, creak, cried, decaf, drake, faced, fader, faked, faker, farce, fared, fibre, fired, freak, fried, irked, raced, raked, backed, backer, barfed, barked, bicker, braced, braked, debark, fabric, faired, racked, bricked, backfire

Puzzle 10

9 Letter Word: Machinery

Other Words: ace, aim, air, any, arc, are, arm, aye, can, car, chi, cry, ear, era, ham, hay, hem, hen, her, hey, hic, hie, him, ice, icy, ire, man, may, men, nay, ram, ran, ray, rim, rye, yam, yen, yin, ache, achy, acme, acne, acre, ahem, airy, amen, arch, army, came, cane, care, chai, char, chia, chin, cram, cyan, each, earn, haem, hair, hare, harm, hear, heir, hire, hymn, inch, mace, main, mane, many, mare, mean, mica, mice, mien, mine, mire, name, narc, nary, near, nice, race, racy, rain, ream, rein, rhea, rice, rich, rime, yarn, yeah, year, chain, chair, charm, chime, china, crane, cream, crime, hairy, harem, hyena, manic, march, mercy, mince, miner, nicer, niche, rainy, ramen, ranch, reach, rhyme, yearn, airmen, cinema, creamy, enrich, hernia, iceman, marine, remain, chimera, chimney, machine, chairmen,

Puzzle 11

9 Letter Word: Operating

Other Words: age, ago, air, ant, ape, apt, are, art, ate, ear, eat, ego, eon, era, gap, get, gin, git, got, ion, ire, nag, nap, net, nit, nor, not, oar, oat, one, opt, ore, pan, par, pat, pea, peg, pen, per, pet, pie, pin, pit, pot, pro, rag, ran, rap, rat, rep, rig, rip, rot, tag, tan, tap, tar, tea, ten, tie, tin, tip, toe, tog, ton, top, anti, atop, earn, ergo, gain, gate, gear, gent, girt, gnat, goat, goer, gone, gore, gran, grin, grip, grit, into, iota, iron, nape, near, neat, noir, nope, nori, note, ogre, open, page, pain, pair, pane, pang, pant, pare, part, pate, pear, peat, pent, pert, pier, pine, ping, pint, pita, poet, pong, pore, port, prat, rage, rain, rang, rant, rape, rapt, rate, reap, rein, rent, ring, riot, ripe, rite, rope, rote, roti, tang, tape, tare, taro, tarp, tear, tier, tire, toga, tone, tong, tore, torn, trap, trio, trip, agent, anger, aping, apron, argon, atone, ergot, gator, genoa, giant, goner, grain, grant, grape, grate, great, gripe, groan, groin, grope, inapt, inept, inert, ingot, inter, intro, irate, nitro, opera, opine, orate, organ, pager, paint, patio, piano, pinot, pinto, point, prang, print, prone, prong, range, ratio, reign, ripen, tango, tapir, tenor, tiger, tinea, tinge, toner, train, tripe, trope, argent, eating, enrapt, entrap, garnet, goitre, gratin, ignore, opiate, opting, orange, orient, ornate, pantie, parent, paring, patron, pigeon, pirate, pointe, protea, raping, rating, ration, regain, region, retain, retina, roping, taping, toeing, toping, triage, granite, ingrate, negator, operant, orating, painter, parting, pertain, pointer, portage, porting, protein, reaping, repaint, tangier, tearing, tapering

Puzzle 12

9 Letter Word: Greatness

Other Words: age, ant, are, art, ate, ear, eat, era, gas, gee, gen, get, nag, nee, net, rag, ran, rat, sag, sat, sea, see, set, tag, tan, tar, tea, tee, ten, ages, ante, ants, arts, earn, ears, ease, east, eats, eras, gate, gear, gees, gene, gent, gets, gnat, gran, nags, near, neat, nest, nets, rage, rags, rang, rant, rate, rats, rent, rest, sage, sags, sane, sang, sans, sate, sear, seas, seat, seen, seer, sees, sent, sets, snag, stag, star, tags, tang, tans, tare, tars, tear, teas, teen, tees, tens, tree, tsar, agent, agree, anger, asset, eager, earns, eases, eaten, eater, enter, erase, gases, gates, gears, genes, genre, gents, gnats, grans, grant, grass, grate, great, green, greet, nears, nests, rages, range, rants, rates, rents, reset, rests, sages, saner, sears, seats, seers, sense, snags, snare, sneer, stage, stags, stare, stars, steer, stern, tangs, tears, tease, teens, tense, trees, tress, tsars, agents, agrees, angers, angsts, argent, assent, assert, eagers, easter, eaters, enrage, enters, erases, esters, garnet, genres, grants, grates, grease, greats, greens, greets, neater, negate, ranges, regent, resent, resets, retags, sateen, seater, senate, snares, sneers, stages, stares, steers, teaser, teases, tenses, argents, earnest, eastern, easters, enrages, grantee, greases, nearest, negater, negates, regents, reseats, restage, seaters, senates, stagers, strange, teasers, assenter, estrange, grantees, negaters, sergeant, estranges, sergeants

Puzzle 13

9 Letter Word: Jabbering

Other Words: age, air, are, bag, ban, bar, beg, bib, big, bin, bra, ear, ebb, era, gib, gin, ire, jab, jag, jar, jig, nab, nag, nib, rag, raj, ran, rib, rig, babe, bane, bang, barb, bare, barn, bean, bear, brag, bran, brie, earn, gain, garb, gear, grab, gran, grin, jean, jibe, near, rage, rain, rang, rein, ring, anger, barge, began, begin, being, binge, brain, bribe, brine, bring, grain, rabbi, range, reign, rejig, baring, binger, ebbing, jabber, jibber, nabber, regain, bearing, jabbing

Puzzle 14

9 Letter Word: Cancelled

Other Words: ace, ale, all, and, can, den, eel, end, lad, lea, led, lee, nee, aced, acne, call, cane, cede, cell, clad, clan, deal, dean, dell, lace, land, lane, lead, lean, lend, need, caned, clean, dance, laced, laden, ladle, lance, called, cancel, candle, celled, lanced, leaned, cadence, cleaned

Puzzle 15

9 Letter Word: Seahorses

Other Words: are, ash, ear, era, has, her, oar, ore, roe, sea, see, she, ears, ease, eras, hare, hear, here, hero, hers, hose, oars, ores, rash, rhea, roes, rose, sash, sear, seas, seer, sees, shoe, soar, sore, arose, ashes, eases, erase, hares, hears, horse, hoses, rheas, roses, sears, seers, share, sheer, shoes, shore, soars, sores, ashore, erases, hearse, heroes, hoarse, horses, rashes, reshoe, sashes, shares, shears, sheers, shores, hearses, reshoes, seahorse, seashore, seashores

Puzzle 16

9 Letter Word: Kangaroos

Other Words: ago, ark, ask, gas, goo, nag, nog, nor, oak, oar, rag, ran, sag, son, arks, goon, gran, nags, nark, nook, oaks, oars, okra, rags, rang, rank, rook, saga, sago, sang, sank, snag, snog, soak, soar, song, sook, soon, agora, argon, arson, goons, grans, groan, narks, okras, organ, ranks, rooks, snark, sonar, angora, anorak, argons, groans, organs, sarong, angoras, anoraks, kangaroo

Puzzle 17

9 Letter Word: Hairspray

Other Words: air, ash, asp, hap, has, hay, hip, his, pay, pry, rap, ray, rip, sap, say, shy, sip, sir, spa, spy, yap, yip, airs, airy, aria, ashy, hair, harp, hays, hips, pair, para, parr, pars, pash, pays, pish, pray, raps, rash, rays, rips, sari, ship, spar, spay, spry, yaps, yips, arias, array, hairs, hairy, harps, harpy, pairs, parry, prays, raspy, sharp, spray, apiary, arrays, pariah, parish, pariahs

Puzzle 18

9 Letter Word: Rainwater

Other Words: air, ant, are, art, ate, awe, ear, eat, era, err, ire, net, new, nit, ran, rat, raw, tan, tar, tea, ten, tie, tin, war, wet, win, wit, anew, ante, anti, area, aria, earn, near, neat, newt, rain, rant, rare, rate, rear, rein, rent, rite, tare, tear, tier, tire, twin, wait, wane, want, ware, warn, wart, wean, wear, weir, went, wine, wire, wren, writ, arena, await, aware, inert, inter, irate, tarre, terra, tiara, tinea, train, trier, trine, twine, water, write, errant, errata, retain, retina, waiter, winter, writer, antiwar, narrate, retrain, terrain, tinware, trainer, warrant, interwar, rainwear

Puzzle 19

9 Letter Word: Daredevil

Other Words: add, aid, ail, air, ale, are, dad, did, die, ear, eel, era, ire, lad, lea, led, lee, lei, lid, lie, rad, red, rid, via, vid, vie, aide, arid, avid, dare, dead, deal, dear, deed, deer, deli, dial, died, dire, diva, dive, earl, eave, ever, evil, idea, idle, laid, lair, lard, lave, lead, leer, liar, lied, live, raid, rail, rave, read, real, reed, reel, ride, rile, vale, veal, veer, veil, vial, vied, vile, adder, addle, aided, ailed, aired, alive, dared, delve, devil, dived, diver, dread, dried, drive, eared, elder, evade, ideal, idled, idler, leave, lever, lived, liver, raved, ravel, revel, riled, rival, valid, velar, viral, dealer, delved, derail, deride, derive, drivel, evaded, evader, ladder, larded, leaded, leader, leaver, levied, raided, railed, redial, relied, relive, reveal, revile, riddle, varied, veiled, vialed, deliver, derived, readied, relived, reviled, deadlier, derailed

Puzzle 20

9 Letter Word: Yardstick

Other Words: act, aid, air, arc, ark, art, ask, car, cat, cry, dak, day, dry, ick, icy, irk, its, kid, kit, rad, rat, ray, rid, sad, sat, say, sic, sir, sit, ski, sky, sty, tad, tar, tic, tis, try, yak, acid, acts, aids, airs, airy, arcs, arid, arks, arts, arty, card, cars, cart, cask, cast, cats, city, cyst, daks, dark, dart, days, dirt, disc, disk, drat, icky, irks, kids, kits, rack, racy, raid, raki, rats, rays, rids, risk, sack, said, saki, sari, scar, scat, sick, skid, skit, star, stay, stir, tack, tars, task, tick, tics, tidy, tray, tsar, yaks, yard, acids, acidy, artsy, cards, carts, dairy, daisy, dart, diary, dirty, ditsy, racks, raids, risky, scary, sitar, skirt, stack, stair, stark, stick, stray, tacks, tacky, tardy, ticks, track, trays, triad, trick, yards, racist, sticky, tracks, triads, tricks, tricky, drastic

Puzzle 21

9 Letter Word: Imposters

Other Words: imp, ire, its, met, mop, opt, ore, per, pet, pie, pit, pot, pro, rep, rim, rip, rot, set, sim, sip, sir, sit, tie, tip, tis, toe, tom, top, emit, imps, item, mess, mire, miso, miss, mist, mite, mope, mops, more, moss, most, omit, opts, ores, perm, pert, pest, pets, pier, pies, pits, poem, poet, pore, port, pose, post, pots, prim, prom, rest, rims, riot, ripe, rips, rise, rite, romp, rope, rose, rote, roti, rots, semi, sets, sips, sire, sirs, site, sits, some, sore, sort, spit, spot, stem, step, stir, stop, temp, term, tier, ties, time, tips, tire, toes, tome, toms, tops, tore, toss, trim, trio, trip, emits, items, merit, metro, miser, mists, mites, mitre, moist, mopes, morse, omits, perms, pesto, pests, piers, poems, poets, poise, pores, ports, poser, poses, posit, posse, posts, press, pries, prime, primo, prism, priss, proms, prose, repot, resit, rests, riots, rises, rites, romps, ropes, roses, rotis, semis, sires, sites, smite, smote, sores, sorts, spies, spire, spite, spits, spore, sport, stems, steps, stirs, stomp, stops, store, storm, strip, tempo, temps, terms, tiers, timer, times, tires, tomes, tress, tries, trims, tripe, trips, trope, import, impose, isomer, merits, metros, misers, mister, mitres, permit, posers, posies, posits, poster, postie, presto, priest, primes, prisms, proses, remiss, repots, resist, simper, sister, smites, sorest, spires, spores, sports, sprite, stomps, stores, storms, stripe, strips, tempos, timers, tripes, tropes, imports, imposer, imposes, impress, isomers, misstep, misters, permits, persist, posters, posties, priests, promise, reposit, rosiest, simpers, sprites, stomper, stories, stripes, imposers, imposter, promises, reposits, stompers, tropisms

Puzzle 22

9 Letter Word: Quadrants

Other Words: and, ant, art, nut, rad, ran, rat, run, rut, sad, sat, sun, tad, tan, tar, urn, ants, aqua, arts, aunt, aura, darn, dart, data, drat, dust, nada, nuts, quad, rant, rats, runs, runt, rust, sand, star, stud, stun, surd, tads, tans, tarn, tars, tsar, tuna, turn, urns, aquas, aunts, auras, darns, darts, daunt, drats, quads, quart, rants, ratan, runts, sauna, squad, squat, stand, trans, tunas, turds, turns, daunts, quarts, quasar, strand, tundra, tundras, quadrant

Puzzle 23

9 Letter Word: Earthling

Other Words: age, ail, air, ale, ant, are, art, ate, ear, eat, era, gel, get, gin, hag, hat, hen, her, hie, hit, ire, lag, lea, leg, lei, let, lie, lit, nag, net, nil, nit, rag, ran, rat, rig, tag, tan, tar, tea, ten, the, tie, tin, ante, anti, earl, earn, gain, gait, gale, gate, gear, gent, girl, girt, glen, glia, gnat, gran, grin, grit, hail, hair, hale, halt, hang, hare, hate, heal, hear, heat, heir, hilt, hint, hire, lain, lair, lane, late, lean, lent, liar, line, lint, nail, near, neat, nigh, rage, rail, rain, rang, rant, rate, real, rein, rent, rile, ring, rite, tail, tale, tang, tare, teal, tear, than, then, thin, tier, tile, tire, agent, agile, aglet, alert, alien, align, alter, angel, anger, angle, earth, eight, giant, girth, glare, glean, glint, gnarl, grail, grain, grant, grate, great, hater, heart, hinge, inert, inlet, irate, large, later, lathe, leant, learn, legit, liger, light, liner, litre, neigh, night, range, regal, reign, relit, renal, right, thane, their, thine, thing, tiger, tiler, tinea, tinge, trail, train, trial, alight, angler, antler, argent, eating, entail, gainer, gaiter, garnet, gather, gelati, genial, gratin, haling, halter, hanger, hating, hernia, inhale, lather, learnt, length, linear, linger, rating, regain, rehang, rental, retail, retain, retina, tailer, tangle, tingle, triage, alright, enthral, granite, hairnet, halting, healing, hearing, heating, ingrate, inhaler, latrine, lighten, lighter, realign, reliant, retinal, ringlet, tagline, tangier, tangler, tearing, alerting, altering, integral, relating, triangle, lathering

Puzzle 24

9 Letter Word: Newsagent

Other Words: age, ant, ate, awe, eat, ewe, gas, gee, get, nag, nan, nee, net, new, sag, sat, saw, sea, see, set, sew, tag, tan, tea, tee, ten, wag, was, wee, wet, ages, anew, ante, ants, awes, ease, east, eats, ewes, gate, gene, gent, gets, gnat, gnaw, nags, nans, neat, nest, nets, news, newt, sage, sane, sang, sate, seat, seen, sent, sewn, snag, stag, stew, swag, swan, swat, tags, tang, tans, teas, teen, tees, tens, wage, wags, wane, want, wean, went, west, wets, agent, angst, eaten, gates, genes, gents, gnats, gnaws, newts, stage, sweat, sweet, tangs, tease, teens, tense, twang, tween, wages, wanes, wants, waste, weans, agents, neaten, negate, newest, sateen, senate, sewage, twangs, tweens, neatens, negates

Puzzle 25

9 Letter Word: Racehorse

Other Words: ace, arc, are, ash, car, cos, ear, era, err, has, her, oar, orc, ore, sac, sea, see, she, aces, ache, acre, arch, arcs, care, cars, case, cash, core, each, ears, ease, echo, eras, errs, hare, hear, here, hero, hers, hose, oars, orca, orcs, ores, race, rare, rash, rear, rhea, roar, rose, scar, sear, seer, shoe, soar, sore, aches, acres, arose, carer, cares, cease, chaos, chars, chase, cheer, chore, chose, cores, crash, erase, hares, hears, horse, ochre, orcas, racer, races, reach, rears, rheas, roars, scare, score, share, shear, sheer, shore, archer, arches, ashore, career, carers, chaser, cheers, chores, coarse, crease, echoes, eraser, hearer, hearse, heroes, hoarse, ochres, racers, reshoe, scorer, search, archers, careers, coarser, hoarser, reaches, shearer, horsecar, research, searcher

Puzzle 26

9 Letter Word: Leftovers

Other Words: eel, elf, eve, fee, foe, for, let, lot, oft, ore, rot, see, set, tee, toe, vet, eels, else, ever, eves, feel, fees, feet, felt, fete, flee, foes, fore, fort, free, fret, leer, left, lest, loft, lore, lose, lost, lots, love, ores, over, reef, reel, rest, role, rose, rote, rots, rove, seer, self, serf, slot, soft, sole, sore, sort, tees, toes, tore, tree, veer, vest, veto, vets, volt, vote, elves, feels, felts, fetes, fever, flees, fleet, forts, frees, frets, frost, leers, lever, lofts, loser, lover, loves, overs, overt, reefs, reels, reset, revel, roles, roves, serve, sever, sleet, solve, steel, steer, stole, store, stove, terse, trees, trove, veers, verse, volts, voter, votes, fester, fevers, fleets, floret, forest, foster, levers, lovers, resole, revels, revolt, softer, solver, stereo, strove, svelte, troves, vetoes, voters, florets, resolve, revolts, leftover

Puzzle 27

9 Letter Word: Sandstone

Other Words: ado, and, ant, ate, den, doe, dot, eat, end, eon, nan, net, nod, not, oat, ode, one, sad, sat, sea, set, sod, son, tad, tan, tea, ted, ten, toe, ton, aeon, ands, anon, ante, ants, date, dean, dens, dent, does, done, dose, dote, dots, east, eats, ends, eons, neat, neon, nest, nets, node, nods, none, nose, note, oats, odes, ones, sand, sane, sans, sate, seas, seat, send, sent, sets, snot, soda, sons, tans, teas, tend, tens, toad, toed, toes, tone, tons, toss, aeons, anode, asset, atone, dates, deans, dents, doses, dotes, nests, nodes, nosed, noses, noted, notes, oaten, onset, sands, sated, sates, seats, sedan, sends, sodas, stand, stead, stone, tends, toads, toned, tones, tonne, anodes, assent, atoned, atones, donate, sanest, season, sedans, sonnet, stands, steads, stoned, stones, tanned, tendon, tonnes, tossed, donates, sonnets, tendons

Puzzle 28

9 Letter Word: Pacemaker

Other Words: ace, amp, ape, arc, are, ark, arm, cap, car, ear, era, map, par, pea, pee, per, ram, rap, acre, area, cake, came, camp, cape, care, carp, cram, keep, maar, mace, make, mare, mark, meek, pace, pack, para, pare, park, peak, pear, peck, peek, peer, perk, perm, pram, race, rack, rake, ramp, rape, ream, reap, reck, reek, caper, cramp, creak, cream, creek, creep, creme, crepe, karma, maker, pacer, parka, peace, recap, ampere, camera, camper, packer, remake, repack, capmaker

Puzzle 29

9 Letter Word: Waistcoat

Other Words: act, cat, cos, cot, cow, oat, sac, sat, saw, sic, sit, sow, tat, tic, tis, tot, tow, two, was, wit, acts, cast, cats, coat, cost, cots, cows, iota, oats, scat, stow, swat, taco, tact, tics, tots, tows, twit, twos, wait, watt, wits, attic, await, coast, coats, iotas, stoat, stoic, tacit, tacos, toast, twats, twist, twits, waist, waits, watts, attics, awaits, static, tatsoi

Puzzle 30

9 Letter Word: Teardrops

Other Words: ado, ape, apt, are, art, asp, ate, doe, dot, ear, eat, era, err, oar, oat, ode, opt, ore, pad, par, pat, pea, per, pet, pod, pot, pro, rad, rap, rat, red, rod, rot, sad, sap, sat, sea, set, sod, spa, tad, tap, tar, tea, toe, top, aped, apes, arts, atop, dare, dart, date, dear, doer, does, dope, dose, dote, dots, drat, drop, ears, east, eats, eras, errs, oars, oats, odes, opts, ores, pads, pare, parr, part, past, pats, pear, peas, peat, pert, pest, pets, pods, poet, pore, port, pose, post, pots, prat, raps, rapt, rare, rasp, rate, rats, read, reap, rear, redo, reds, rest, road, roar, rode, rods, rope, rort, rose, rote, rots, sate, sear, seat, soap, soar, soda, sore, sort, spar, spat, sped, spot, star, step, stop, tape, taps, tare, taro, tarp, tars, tear, teas, toad, toed, toes, tops, tore, trap, trod, tsar, adept, adopt, adore, arose, darer, dares, darts, dates, dears, doers, dopes, dotes, drape, drops, oared, opera, opted, orate, order, pared, pares, parse, parts, paste, pears, peats, pesto, poets, pored, pores, ports, posed, poser, prose, rated, rates, reads, reaps, rears, retro, roads, roars, roast, roped, ropes, sated, spade, spare, spate, spear, spore, sport, stare, stead, store, strap, taped, taper, tapes, tared, tares, tarps, tears, tepas, terra, toads, trade, traps, tread, trope, adopts, adores, arrest, depart, deport, draper, drapes, operas, orated, orates, orders, parrot, parsed, parted, pasted, pastor, ported, porter, posted, poster, presto, protea, raptor, rarest, rasped, report, repots, resort, roared, roster, sapote, soaped, soared, sorted, sorter, spared, spored, spread, stared, stored, storer, strode, tapers, trader, trades, treads, tropes, adopter, adorers, departs, deports, drapers, eardrop, parrots, porters, raptors, reports, roasted, roaster, seaport, sparred, sported, starred, traders, adopters, eardrops, parroted, predator, roadster, teardrop, predators

Enjoy this Bonus Word Find!

Did Shakespeare Write That?

```
A Q T X V B H E N R Y V I I I G D Y K T
K S X P O L I G W V I P U P O U T I I A
U F C Y M B E L I N E O T H E L L O N S
F O U U H Z F C O R I O L A N U S D G Y
G S T L O V E S L A B O R L O S T T L O
H R L T P V G R U O V V D D R D P M E U
E P O J T A A G U B F W D O E N H O A L
N K T M H N D W M Q J Y U Q V U S L R I
R I T Q E Q X R L U C R E C E A C F Y K
Y N R Q T O W P K I D M A C B E T H V E
V G N E E S A Z J C R I C H A R D I I I
H J K C M W I N T E R S T A L E U T W T
A O N Y P A G G D T V T W S O N N E T S
M H L Q E O B W M J R G U Z O U W O S U
L N M E S C Z X B W U N Y E K P F D J C
E L D P T W G N N Y Z L T B G L L X F Z
T P G Q J C E J H P E R I C L E S F Q S
A L V J L T B I Z R P H S E H B K B F A
T W E L F T H N I G H T D P T L E O G F
A E F L A R G J U L I U S C A E S A R I
```

AS YOU LIKE IT	HENRY VIII	LUCRECE	ROMEO AND JULIET
CORIOLANUS	JULIUS CAUSAR	MARCBETH	SONNETS
CYMBELINE	KING JOHN	OTHELLO	THE TEMPEST
HAMLET	KING LEAR	PERICLES	TWELTH NIGHT
HENRY V	LOVES LABOR LOST	RICHARD II	WINTERS TALE

Looking for more word puzzles?

Why not check out Word Finds Volume 1

Available at www.sneakyuniverse.com/store

www.ingramcontent.com/pod-product-compliance
Lightning Source LLC
Chambersburg PA
CBHW071547080526
44588CB00011B/1821